Quick-Cut Basket Quilts

Sharon Cerny Ogden

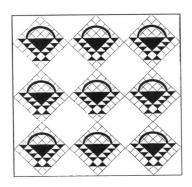

DOVER PUBLICATIONS, INC.
Mineola, New York

Copyright

Copyright © 1998 by Sharon Cerny Ogden
All rights reserved under Pan American and International Copyright Conventions.

Published in Canada by General Publishing Company, Ltd., 30 Lesmill Road, Don Mills, Toronto, Ontario.
Published in the United Kingdom by Constable and Company, Ltd., 3 The Lanchesters, 162–164 Fulham Palace Road, London W6 9ER.

Bibliographical Note

Quick-Cut Basket Quilts is a new work, first published by Dover Publications, Inc., in 1998.

Library of Congress Cataloging-in-Publication Data

Ogden, Sharon Cerny.
    Quick-cut basket quilts / Sharon Cerny Ogden.
        p.   cm.
    ISBN 0-486-29911-2 (pbk.)
    1. Patchwork—Patterns. 2. Patchwork quilts. 3. Baskets in art.
I. Title.
TT835.02823   1998
746.46'041—dc21   97-46415
                                                                 CIP

Manufactured in the United States of America
Dover Publications, Inc., 31 East 2nd Street, Mineola, N. Y. 11501

Introduction

Baskets have been a popular design motif ever since American women began quilting. Early baskets were generally cut from printed chintz or constructed separately and appliquéd to the quilt top. The pieced variety of the pattern made its first appearance somewhere between 1850 and 1875. Basket quilts have even been documented among possessions brought along the Oregon Trail, which was traveled between 1840 and 1870. In early years, patterns for basket quilts were probably sold at fairs and traded among quiltmakers long before the designs were commercially available. Baskets continue to be pieced and appliquéd in every imaginable form even today.

During the Depression, basket quilts were sometimes made using "feed sacks." Flour, sugar, corn meal, salt, tobacco, and potatoes, among other things, often came in sacks made of coarse muslin printed with floral or geometric patterns. After the bags were emptied and washed, much of the fabric remained usable and found its way into quilts of the period.

Basket quilts were often made as "scrap" quilts with a muslin background which made the basket designs "float" on the fabric. These designs are still intriguing to the quilter today. With the instructions in this book, you will learn how to "quick cut and piece" patched baskets. Many ideas for quilt sets are given, as well as full instructions on determining the yardage needed for your very own quilt. Many of the quilt sets show beautiful secondary patterns. I've always been fascinated with the many different ways a quilt block can be set in a top.

The designs are organized into 4-, 5-, 6-, and 7-patch blocks for easy reference. My goal for this book was to take some intricate pieced basket designs and make them easier to tackle. I hope I have accomplished this, not only with the blocks themselves, but also with the fabric calculations. Learning how to easily calculate fabric requirements will make almost any design adaptable to your quilt.

My hope is that you will be inspired to experiment with your own quilt sets and produce your own "basket-inspired" quilt. Happy quilting!

Sharon Cerny Ogden

Beginning Your Quilt

Once you have read through or looked through the whole book, you are ready to decide which block and set you want to use for your quilt. Here's how to begin.

1. Choose a block—pages 13–29.

2. Measure your bed and decide on an overall size for your quilt. Do you want the quilt to just cover the mattress and use a dust ruffle or do you want it to reach the floor? See page 6 for standard mattress size and common sizes of commercially made quilts.

3. Decide on the block size and calculate the number of blocks required—page 7.

4. Calculate how much fabric you will need—page 7.

5. Quick-cut and piece your triangle-squares and plain squares—pages 4–5.

6. Construct the individual blocks—page 6.

7. "Set" the blocks together—pages 8–9.

8. Finish your quilt—page 10.

General Instructions

Quick-Cutting and Piecing Right Triangles

First, determine what size you want the finished square (containing two right triangles) to be, then add 1" to this size. For example, for a 2" finished square, add one whole inch, making 3".

Lay the two fabrics to be used in your pieced triangle-squares with right sides together, with the light-colored fabric on top. It is best to work with fabric no larger than 18" by 22". I like using "fat quarters" to draw and cut my triangle-squares. This is an easy and economical size to work on.

Using a reliable see-through ruler and a pencil, begin by marking horizontal lines 3" apart on the wrong side of the light-colored fabric (*Fig. 1*).

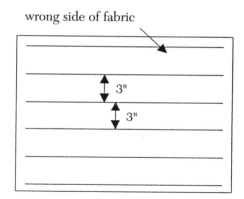

Fig. 1.

Next, mark vertical lines perpendicular to the horizontal lines, forming a grid of 3" squares on the wrong side of the lighter fabric (*Fig. 2*). Be sure that your squares are truly square by using a perfect right triangle to draw the vertical lines perpendicular to the horizontal lines.

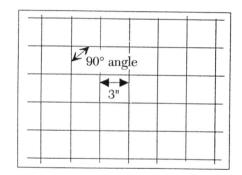

Fig. 2.

Next, you will draw diagonal lines through the corners of all the squares (*Fig. 3*).

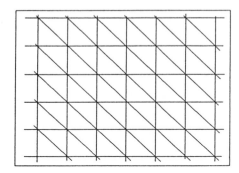

Fig. 3.

Now you are ready to sew. Using a ¼" seam allowance, sew along both sides of every diagonal line (*Fig. 4*).

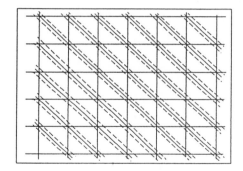

Fig. 4.

After you have sewn all the lines, cut the sewn pieces apart, cutting on every drawn line, horizontal, vertical, and diagonal (*Fig. 5*). You will get two identical units from every grid square drawn. You will find that you have sewn a few stitches across the corners of most of the squares; these can be easily removed by picking them out with a seam ripper or a pin.

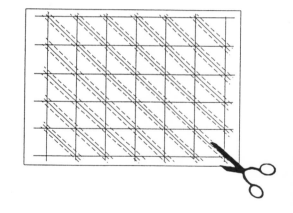

Fig. 5.

Press the seam allowance to the dark side (*Fig. 6*) before using the pieced squares in any blocks.

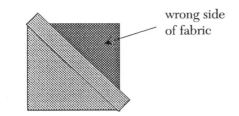

Fig. 6.

wrong side of fabric

After pressing, trim away the points that extend beyond the square (*Fig. 7*), and you are ready to use your pieced squares in any one of the basket blocks.

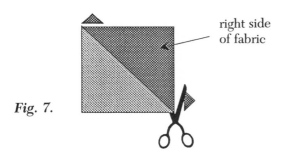

right side of fabric

Fig. 7.

For each of the blocks shown in this book there is a chart indicating how many pieced squares are required. Just multiply the number of pieced squares you need for each block by the number of blocks in your quilt. Mark and sew enough fabric pieces to cut all of the pieced squares for your quilt. Don't worry about piecing the exact number of needed squares. It is better to have too many than too few.

Other quick-piecing methods can be employed when making your quilt. For instance, if the block has multiple squares pieced together, cut a strip of each fabric ½" wider than the finished square (*Fig. 8*), then sew these long strips together using a ¼" seam

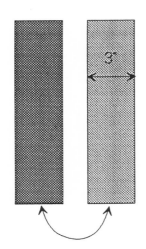

Fig. 8.

allowance. After they are joined, mark each with cutting lines the same distance apart as the width of the original strips (*Fig. 9*); cut along these lines. The result is joined squares (*Fig. 10*).

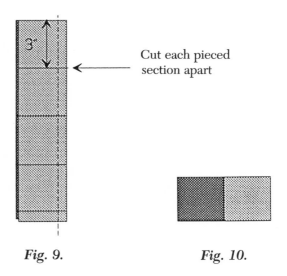

Cut each pieced section apart

Fig. 9.   *Fig. 10.*

This method can also be used to piece several strips together at once (*Fig. 11*). Cut the strips apart to form smaller strips (*Fig. 12*). These smaller strips can be then be pieced together into blocks (*Fig. 13*).

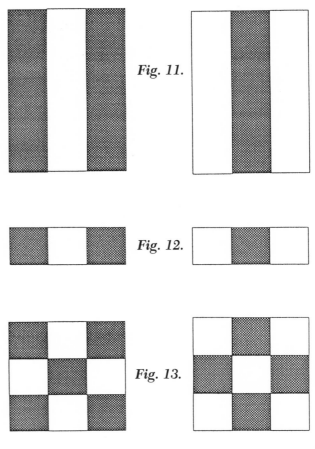

Fig. 11.

Fig. 12.

Fig. 13.

Block Construction

Once you have quick cut and pieced all of your squares and triangle-squares, you must join them. Following the diagram shown with each block, arrange the triangle-squares and squares (*Fig. 14*). Sew the patches together to form rows (*Fig. 15*), then sew the rows together to complete the block (*Fig. 16*).

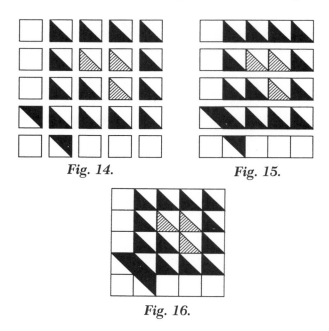

Fig. 14.   Fig. 15.

Fig. 16.

Determining the Size of Your Quilt

To determine the finished size for your quilt, start with the dimensions (length and width) of the mattress. Add 8" to 12" to the length if you want a pillow tuck. Then decide how much of a drop is needed on each side. To figure out the drop, measure from the top of the mattress to just below the top of the dust ruffle (or to the floor). For most quilts, you will add this "drop" once to the length (for the bottom of the bed) and twice to the width (once for each side). Also, you will want to add 2" to 3" to both the length and width of your quilt for the amount taken up by your quilting.

NOTE: Mattress pads, sheets, and blankets will add inches to the measurements, so be sure to measure the mattress and drop when you have bedding on the bed.

Standard Mattress Sizes

Mattresses are made in standard sizes. The size of waterbed mattresses may vary slightly. Also, the depth of your mattress may vary, so measuring the bed for which you are making the quilt is very important.

CHART 1. Standard mattress sizes

Crib	27" x 52"
Youth	33" x 66"
Twin	39" x 74"
Full	54" x 74"
Queen	60" x 80"
King	78" x 80"

Commercial Measurements

Most commercially bought bed coverings (whether they are comforters, blankets or bedspreads) come in some "standard" sizes. Unfortunately, these sizes can also vary as much as 6". I've included these dimensions as a guideline for you in determining the finished size of your quilt.

Comforters (which I use as a term for a bed covering that is generally designed to be used as a blanket) usually cover the mattress with a little extra to spare. They don't always cover the box spring or allow for a pillow tuck. They could be used with a dust ruffle without covering the pillows. Pillow shams can be used, or a pillow covering.

CHART 2. Comforter sizes

Twin	66" x 86"
Full	76" x 86"
Queen	86" x 88"
King	102" x 88"

Bedspreads cover the bed and fall almost to the floor if the top of the mattress is the standard 20"–21" from the floor, and allow for a pillow tuck.

CHART 3. Bedspread sizes

Twin	80" x 108"
Full	96" x 108"
Queen	102" x 118"
King	120" x 118"

Adapting a Design to a Different Size

If the quilt you want to make is not the desired finished size, there are several things you can do to adjust the design.

To make a quilt smaller, eliminate a row of blocks,

set the blocks without sashing, and/or narrow the border strips.

For a larger quilt, make an extra row or two of blocks, add sashing, widen sashing, and/or add multiple borders. But remember, each addition will require additional fabric which must be calculated.

Determining the Number of Blocks Required

Decide on the overall size of the quilt. Pick a quilt block and a quilt block size.

For straight sets, divide the size of the block into the width of the quilt, then into the length of the quilt. For example, for a 90" x 120" quilt with a 10" block, divide 90" by 10", then 120" by 10". Your quilt will be 9 blocks by 12 blocks. With a 15" block, the quilt with be 6 blocks by 8 blocks (90"/15" = 6; 120"/15" = 8).

If, when you calculate the number of blocks required for your quilt, you end up with a remainder, use the whole number, then add the appropriate width border, i.e., 96"/15" block = 6.4 blocks. Use 6 blocks with a 3" border on each side. 120"/15" block = 8 blocks. You could either add a 3" border top and bottom, making your quilt 126" (which could be used for a pillow tuck), or have borders only on the sides.

Calculating Fabric Requirements

Multiply the number of combination triangle-squares needed per block (see the individual block instructions and the chart on page 31) by the number of blocks required.

Using Chart 4 below, determine how many pieced squares can be cut from each 18" x 22" unit (two fabric pieces with right sides together). Remember, you will get two pieced squares from each drawn square.

A rough way to calculate the amount of fabric needed is to determine how much is needed for the back of the quilt, double it for the front, and divide it among the fabrics used. For instance, in the New York Basket (page 27), approximately one-half of the fabric used is light, one quarter is medium and one quarter is dark. A 40" by 60" quilt would require 60" of 45"-wide fabric for the back. Using the above formula, the front would require approximately 120"–60" of light and 30" each of medium and dark. If the fabrics are all used equally, you can divide by the number of fabrics.

Borders and stripping (sashing) should be cut across the width of the fabric. It is important to calculate how many strips you will need to cut for your borders before cutting the rest of your fabric.

Here's an example. If you have an 86" x 100" quilt that will have a 5" border all around, you would need 86" + 86" + 100" + 100", or 372" of 5½"-wide fabric. I use 40" as an assumed fabric width (this allows for shrinkage), therefore, you would need to cut ten 5½" strips of fabric. This is 55", or 1⅝ yards of fabric for the border. See how easy that was!

If you are planning a double border (3" and 4") for the same 86" x 100" quilt, here's how to calculate: 86" – 4" – 4" = 78"; 100" – 4" – 4" = 92".

The 3" inner border would require 78" + 78" + 92"+ 92" = 340" of 3½"-wide fabric or 9 strips. This equals 31½" (I'd buy a yard).

The 4" outer border would require 86" + 86" + 100" + 100", or 372" of 4½"-wide fabric or 10 strips. This equals 45"—purchase at least 1⅜" yards to allow for shrinkage and straightening.

CHART 4. Number of triangle squares from each 18" x 22" unit

Finished size	Grid size	Grid layout	Yield
2"	3"	5 x 6	60 pieced squares
2½"	3½"	4 x 5	40 pieced squares
3"	4"	4 x 4	32 pieced squares
3½"	4½"	3 x 4	24 pieced squares
4"	5"	3 x 3	18 pieced squares
4½"	5½"	3 x 3	18 pieced squares
5"	6"	2 x 3	12 pieced squares
5½"	6½"	2 x 2	8 pieced squares
6"	7"	2 x 2	8 pieced squares

Quilt Sets

The way the quilt blocks are arranged within a quilt is referred to as the "set." There are several different ways to set a quilt together.

Straight Set with No Sashing (*Fig. 17*)

The simplest way to join the blocks is to sew them together directly. Often, when quilts are joined this way, a "secondary" pattern is formed where the block designs meet. Many of the blocks in this book are shown in this type of set. The quilt size is number of blocks across or down times the block size.

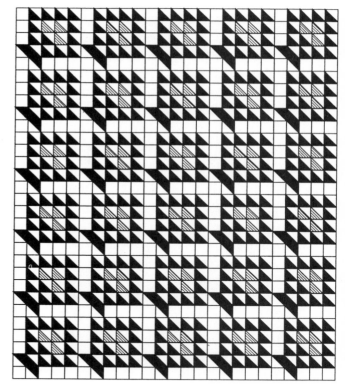

Fig. 17.

Straight Set with Alternate Blocks (*Fig. 18*)

In this set, the pieced blocks are alternated with plain blocks. In such a quilt set, the pattern works best if the number of blocks across is an uneven number. The number of rows down can be either an even or odd number.

CHART 5. Sizes of a quilt 5 blocks x 5 blocks

10" block	50" x 50" quilt
12½" block	62½" x 62½" quilt
15" block	75" x 75" quilt
17½" block	87½" x 87½" quilt
20" block	100" x 100" quilt

Just by lengthening the quilt by two rows, you can come close to quilt size for a bed.

CHART 6. Sizes of a quilt 5 blocks x 7 blocks

10" block	50" x 70" quilt
12½" block	62½" x 87½" quilt
15" block	75" x 105" quilt
17½" block	87½" x 122½" quilt
20" block	100" x 140" quilt

Fig. 18.

Straight Set with Sashing (*Fig. 19*)

Quilt blocks can also be joined with sashing. In this instance, using 4" sashing, a quilt 4 blocks by 4 blocks will yield the following:

CHART 7. Sizes of a quilt 5 x 5 blocks with 4" sashing

10" block	74" x 74" quilt
12½" block	86½" x 86½" quilt
15" block	99" x 99" quilt
17½" block	111½" x 111½" quilt
20" block	124" x 124" quilt

Lengthen the quilt by one row and once again you are close to bed size:

CHART 8. Sizes of a quilt 5 x 6 blocks with 4" sashing

10" block	74" x 88" quilt
12½" block	86½" x 103" quilt
15" block	99" x 118" quilt
17½" block	111½" x 133" quilt
20" block	124" x 148" quilt

Diagonal Sets (*Fig. 20*)

All of the quilt sets discussed above can be set on the diagonal by turning the blocks 45°. You commonly see sets without sashing and sets with alternate blocks arranged this way. The edges and corners of such a set are filled out with half- and quarter-blocks. For sets on the bias, there is a very simple way to create templates for the plain blocks. First decide on the actual block size. Draw that onto plastic, divide it diagonally in both directions (*Fig. 21*). Use ¼ of the template for the quarter pieces and half the template for the half-size pieces. Don't forget to add ¼" seam allowance to all edges. To figure the size for these quilts, you must measure the block from corner to corner. Borders can be added to bring the quilt to an appropriate size.

CHART 9. Sizes of a quilt 3 blocks x 4 blocks

Block size	Diagonal measurement	Approximate Quilt Size
10"	14⅛"	42⅜" x 56½"
12½"	17⅝"	52⅞" x 70½"
15"	21¼"	63¾" x 85"
17½"	24¾"	74¼" x 99"
20"	28¼"	84¾" x 113"

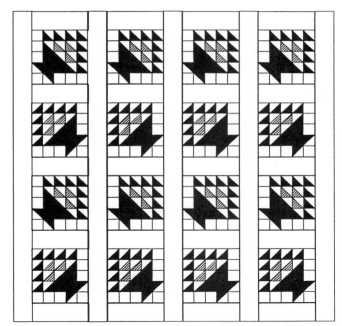

Fig. 19.

Fig. 20.

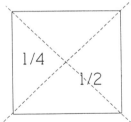

Fig. 21.

Finishing Your Quilt

The quilt back should be 3" to 4" larger than your quilt top in both length and width. Depending on the size of your quilt, you will probably have to join lengths of fabric for the backing.

To assemble the quilt, place the backing, wrong side up, on your work surface. Spread the batting over the backing and smooth it out; center the quilt top, right side up, on top of the batting. Pin the three layers together with long quilter's pins. With white thread, baste every 6" both horizontally and vertically. Remove the pins and you are ready to quilt.

Often a piece to be quilted is placed in a frame or hoop to keep the layers taut as you work. The choice is yours as to whether or not to use a frame or a hoop.

The quilting stitch is a simple running stitch worked through all three layers. Your stitches should all be equal in length and should be the same length on the front and the back of your quilt. It is easiest to quilt toward your body. Your thread should be no longer than 18" to reduce twisting and knotting as you work.

After all the quilting is finished, trim the top, batt, and backing evenly. Bind the quilt or turn in the edges of the top and backing ¼" and slipstitch together.

4-Patch Baskets

All of the finished squares in the blocks are the same size.

Block size	Each finished square	Drawn square
10" block	2½"	3½"
12" block	3"	4"
14" block	3½"	4½"
16" block	4"	5"
18" block	4½"	5½"
20" block	5"	6"

Flower Pot #1

For each block in your quilt, prepare the following quick-cut and pieced triangle-squares:

10 dark/light combinations

1 medium/light combination

Cut the following number of plain squares (cut ½" larger than the desired finished size):

5 light

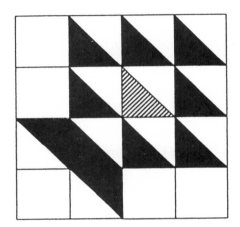

Bread Basket

For each block in your quilt, prepare the following quick-cut and pieced triangle-squares:

3 dark/light combinations

2 dark/medium combinations

2 medium/light combinations

Cut the following number of plain squares (cut ½" larger than the desired finished size):

8 light

1 medium

Cut 1 handle to appliqué onto the block.

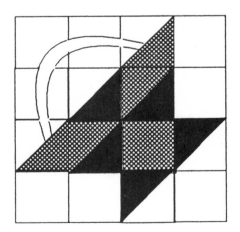

Tea Basket

For each block in your quilt, prepare the following quick-cut and pieced triangle-squares:

1 dark/light combination

4 medium/light combinations

2 medium/dark combinations

Cut the following number of plain squares (cut ½" larger than the desired finished size):

5 light

4 dark

Cut 1 dark stem to appliqué onto the completed block.

Flower Pot #1
4-Patch Basket

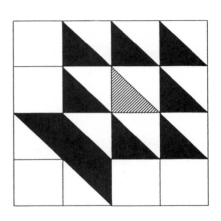

Note the delightful secondary design formed when the quilt blocks are set as below. This setting requires an even number of rows and columns.

Bread Basket
4-Patch Basket

The handles are appliquéd onto the block after it is put together. The easiest way to make a template for the handle is to take a large round dish and use it to draw your semi-circular handle. Then sketch about ¾" from that drawn edge for the inside of the handle.

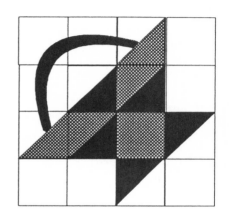

Tea Basket

4-Patch Basket

The rectangular "stem" of the tea basket is appliquéd onto the block when the block is finished.

In order for the secondary design to work with this layout, you must have an even number of rows and an even number of columns.

This layout would work with either an odd or even number of rows and columns.

5-Patch Baskets

All of the finished squares in the blocks are the same size.

Block size	Each finished square	Drawn square
10" block	2"	3"
12½" block	2½"	3½"
15" block	3"	4"
20" block	4"	5"

Grape Basket

For each block in your quilt, prepare the following quick-cut and pieced triangle-squares:

4 dark/light combinations

11 medium/light combinations

Cut the following number of plain squares (cut ½" larger than the desired finished size):

9 light

1 dark

Cake Stand

For each block in your quilt, prepare the following quick-cut and pieced triangle-squares:

5 dark/light combinations

6 medium/light combinations

Cut the following number of plain squares (cut ½" larger than the desired finished size):

11 light

3 dark

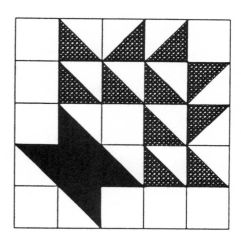

Fruit Basket

For each block in your quilt, prepare the following quick-cut and pieced triangle-squares:

7 medium/light combinations

3 dark/medium combinations

2 dark/light combinations

Cut the following number of plain squares (cut ½" larger than the desired finished size):

7 light

3 medium

3 dark

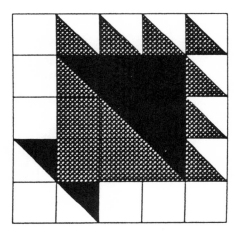

Flower Pot #2

For each block in your quilt, prepare the following quick-cut and pieced triangle-squares:

12 dark/light combinations

3 medium/light combinations

Cut the following number of plain squares (cut ½" larger than the desired finished size):

7 light

3 dark

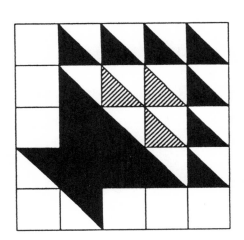

Flower Pot #3

For each block in your quilt, prepare the following quick-cut and pieced triangle-squares:

5 light/dark combinations

1 medium #1/dark combination

1 medium #1/light combination

1 medium #2/dark combination

1 medium #2/light combination

1 medium #3/dark combination

1 medium #3/light combination

Cut the following number of plain squares (cut ½" larger than the desired finished size):

8 light

6 dark

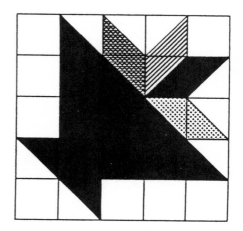

Grandmother's Basket

For each block in your quilt, prepare the following quick-cut and pieced triangle-squares:

6 dark/light combinations

6 medium/dark combinations

Cut the following number of plain squares (cut ½" larger than the desired finished size):

13 light

1 handle to appliqué onto the completed block

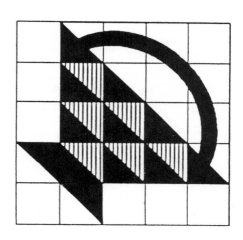

18

Grape Basket
5-Patch Basket

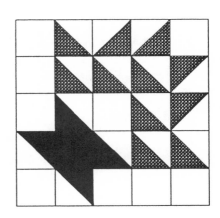

When the setting is done as below, and the fabric used for the plain block is similar to the fabric used for the background of the pieced block, the baskets seem to "float" on the quilt.

Cake Stand
5-Patch Basket—View 1

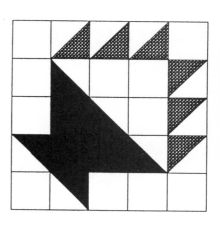

Again, in this setting, a beautiful secondary design appears as the blocks are put together. This setting requires an even number of rows and columns.

Cake Stand
5-Patch Basket—View 2

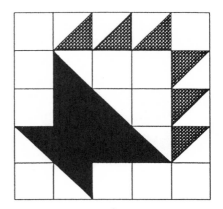

What a dramatic difference there is when you add simple stripping between the blocks.

Fruit Basket

5-Patch Basket

You will notice that the Fruit Basket is similar to the Cake Stand, however, the inside of the handle is a different fabric than the background fabric in this design. Also note the different rotation of the triangles in the handles. This is another setting that requires even numbers of rows and columns for the secondary design to appear.

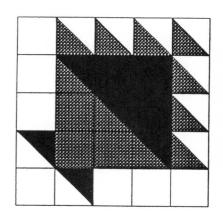

Flower Pot #2

5-Patch Basket

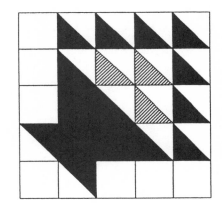

Flower Pot #3

5-Patch Basket

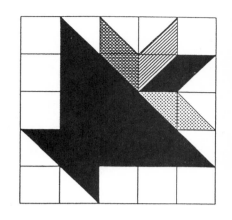

6-Patch Baskets

All of the finished squares in the blocks are the same size.

Block size	Each finished square	Drawn square
12" block	2"	3"
15" block	2½"	3½"
18" block	3"	4"
21" block	3½"	4½"

New York Basket

For each block in your quilt, prepare the following quick-cut and pieced triangle-squares:

3 light/medium combinations

10 dark/light combinations

Cut the following number of plain squares (cut ½" larger than the desired finished size):

20 light

3 medium

1 handle to appliqué onto the completed block

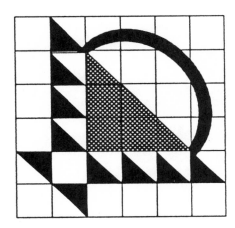

Cherry Basket

For each block in your quilt, prepare the following quick-cut and pieced triangle-squares:

2 light/medium combinations

10 medium/dark combinations

5 dark/light combinations

Cut the following number of plain squares (cut ½" larger than the desired finished size):

19 light

1 handle to appliqué onto the completed block

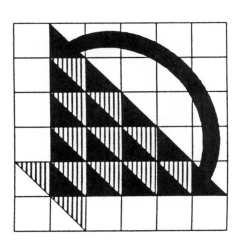

New York Basket

6-Patch Basket

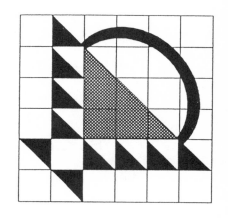

Cherry Basket
6-Patch Basket

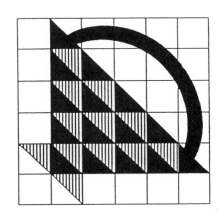

A "plain" or "straight" set as shown below can be accomplished with either an odd or even number of rows and columns.

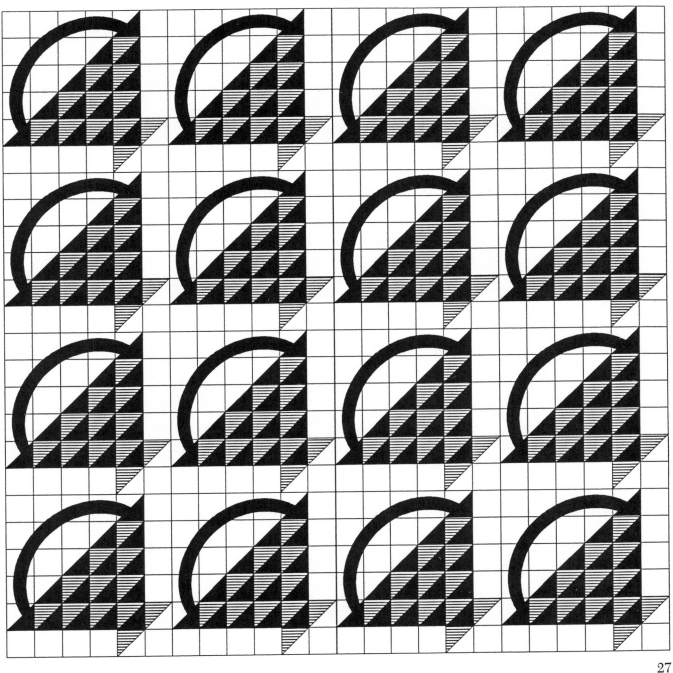

7-Patch Basket

All of the finished squares in the blocks are the same size.

Block size	Each finished square	Drawn square
14" block	2"	3"
17½" block	2½"	3½"
21" block	3"	4"

Basket of Flowers

For each block in your quilt, prepare the following quick-cut and pieced triangle-squares:

16 dark/light combinations

Cut the following number of plain squares (cut ½" larger than the desired finished size):

33 light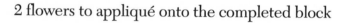

2 flowers to appliqué onto the completed block

1 handle to appliqué onto the completed block

Basket of Flowers
7-Patch Basket

An easy way to make a template for the flowers is to take a spool and draw 5 overlapping circles onto plastic template material. Use a smaller spool for the flower center. The flowers and handle are appliquéd.

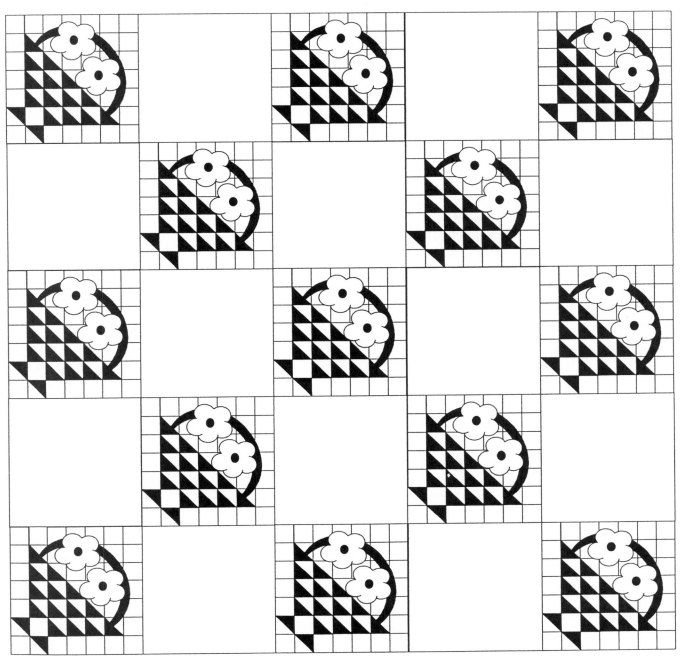

A Smaller Basket Project

Now that you are interested in basket quilts, why not try out quick-cutting and piecing on a small project first, by making a table runner for your table.

Choose any one of the basket blocks, then decide on a block size (the bigger the table, the bigger the block should be).

Make two blocks using the quick-cutting and piecing instructions in this book. Following the instructions on page 11 for cutting quarter fill-in triangles, cut four fill-in triangles (*Fig. 1*).

Cut a rectangular piece the length required for your table. Sew the two basket blocks (with the fill-in triangles already added) onto the rectangle (*Fig. 2*). Using the completed runner as a pattern, cut a back and batting. Layer the batting, the back (right side up), and the top (right side down). Pin and sew ¼" from the edge, leaving about 4" open along ones edge. Turn right side out, slip-stitch opening and quilt. It's as easy as that!.

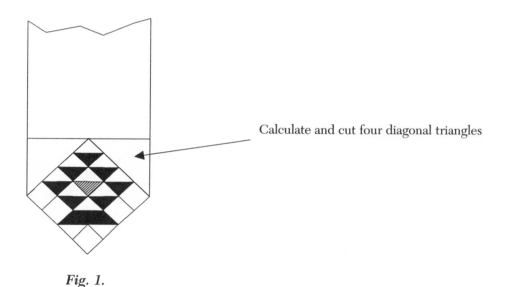

Calculate and cut four diagonal triangles

Fig. 1.

Fig. 2.

Cutting Charts for Basket Blocks

	Block	No. of Dark/Light Triangles	No. of Med. #1/Dark Triangles	No. of Med. #2/Dark Triangles	No. of Med. #3/Dark Triangles	No. of Med. #1/Light	No. of Med. #2/Light	No. of Med. #3/Light Triangles	No. of squares cut .5" larger than			Total No. of Squares per Block
									Dark	Medium	Light	
4-Patch Basket Block	Flower Pot #1	10	0	0	0	1	0	0	0	0	5	16
	Bread Basket	3	2	0	0	2	0	0	0	1	8	16
	Tea Basket	1	2	0	0	4	0	0	4	0	8	16
5-Patch Basket Block	Fruit Basket	2	3	0	0	7	0	0	3	3	7	25
	Grape Basket	11	0	0	0	4	0	0	1	0	9	25
	Cake Stand	5	0	0	0	6	0	0	3	0	11	25
	Flower Pot #2	12	0	0	0	3	0	0	3	0	7	25
	Flower Pot #3	5	1	1	1	1	1	1	6	0	8	25
	Grandmother's Basket	6	6	0	0	0	0	0	0	0	13	25
6-Patch Basket Block	Cherry Basket	5	10	0	0	2	0	0	0	0	19	36
	New York Basket	10	0	0	0	3	0	0	0	3	20	36
7-Patch Basket Block	Basket of Flowers	16	0	0	0	0	0	0	0	0	33	49

About the Author

Sharon Cerny Ogden, quilt teacher and historian, is noted for her quick-piecing and sewing methods. A quilter for over 20 years, she has published articles in *The Professional Quilter* magazine on quilt retailing and teaching and in *The Chronicle of the Early American Industries Association* on quilt history. She was the editor of the *Long Island Antique Bottle Association Newsletter,* and currently is editor of the *Lancaster Goat Connection.* She is the author of two previous Dover books, *Irish Chain Quilts: Single, Double and Triple* (1992) and *Optical Illusions Quilt Designs* (1994). Sharon also owned and operated a quilt shop, The Gingerbread House in Farmingdale, New York for five years. In 1986, she was nominated "Quilt Teacher of the Year" by *The Professional Quilter* magazine.

More recently, Sharon has pursued her career in quilting along a different path. Dressed in authentically detailed reproduction clothing, using quilts, samplers, and coverlets, she tells the story of the life of a woman in the 1850s and the hardships she might face.

Along with her husband, Oliver, she travels throughout America performing this presentation for historical organizations, living-history museums, genealogy societies, retirement homes, and church groups. Some of the living-history museums that have hosted this presentation are Landis Valley Farm Museum in Lancaster, Pennsylvania, Old Economy Village in Ambridge, Pennsylvania, New Harmony Historical Site in New Harmony, Indiana, The Museums at Stony Brook, Stony Brook, New York, Scott-Fanton Museum in Danbury, Connecticut, and Somerset Historical Center in Somerset, Pennsylvania.

Sharon and Oliver have a dairy goat farm and now reside in Lancaster, Pennsylvania. Sharon still quilts and recently completed for her parents' church, a funeral pall of gold and white chintz in memory of her father. Quilts are still a priority and new designs are always a challenge. Living on a farm has also prompted her to experiment with some animal patchwork designs.